Habitats

Deserts

Andrea Rivera

abdopublishing.com

Published by Abdo Zoom, a division of ABDO, P.O. Box 398166, Minneapolis, Minnesota 55439.

Copyright © 2018 by Abdo Consulting Group, Inc. International copyrights reserved in all countries.

No part of this book may be reproduced in any form without written permission from the publisher.

Printed in the United States of America, North Mankato, Minnesota.

092017

012018

THIS BOOK CONTAINS
RECYCLED MATERIALS

Photo Credits: iStock, Shutterstock

Production Contributors: Kenny Abdo, Jennie Forsberg, Grace Hansen, John Hansen

Design Contributors: Dorothy Toth, Neil Klinepier

Publisher's Cataloging-in-Publication Data

Names: Rivera, Andrea, author.

Title: Deserts / by Andrea Rivera.

Description: Minneapolis, Minnesota: Abdo Zoom, 2018. | Series: Habitats |
    Includes online resource and index.

Identifiers: LCCN 2017939225 | ISBN 9781532120640 (lib.bdg.) | ISBN 9781532121760 (ebook) |
    ISBN 9781532122323 (Read-to-Me ebook)

Subjects: LCSH: Deserts--Juvenile literature. | Biomes--Juvenile literature. | Habitats--Juvenile literature.

Classification: DDC 577.54--dc23

LC record available at https://lccn.loc.gov/2017939225

Table of Contents

Deserts are a kind of habitat. They are very dry. Most are also very hot.

Special animals and plants live in this habitat.

A camel stores fat in its hump.
A cactus can store water.

Many reptiles also live in the desert. Desert iguanas love the sun and heat!

Technology

Deserts are often very sunny.

People set up solar panels in deserts. Solar panels convert the sun's rays into thermal or electrical energy.

Solar power is a very clean form of renewable energy. It is also the most abundant.

Engineering

Desert homes provide shelter from the heat.

Adobe is often used for building in the desert. Homes also have thick walls. This helps keep them cool.

Art

Ancient art has been found in deserts. Paintings and engravings were found on rocks in the Sahara Desert. They are thousands of years old.

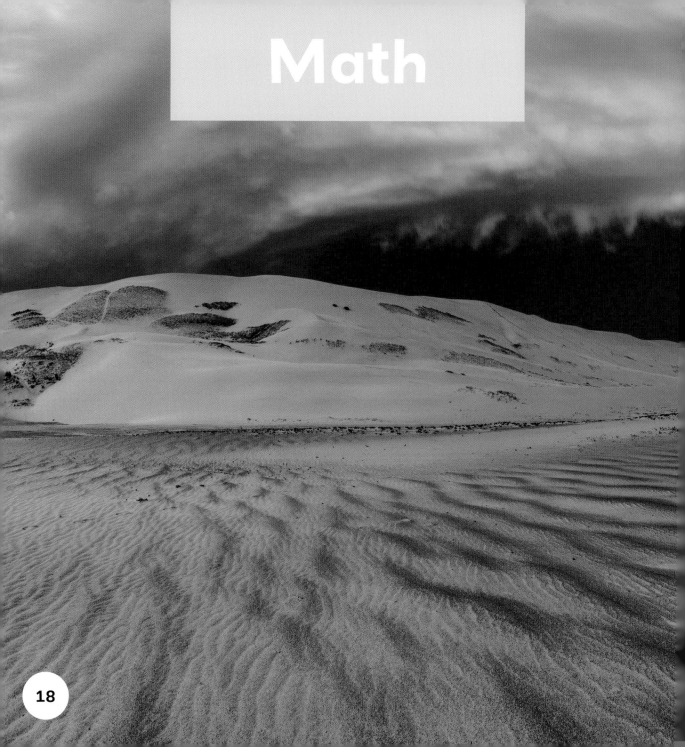

Math

Rain is rare in deserts. Deserts get less than 10 inches (25 cm) of rain each year. Some areas have not seen rain in 100 years!

Key Stats

- Deserts cover about one-fifth of Earth's surface.

- The Sahara Desert in Africa is the world's largest desert. It covers more than 3 million square miles (8,000,000 sq. km).

- Death Valley is a desert in the United States. It is one of the hottest places on Earth. It reached 134°F (57°C) in 1913.

Glossary

abundant – more than enough.

adobe – clay mixed with straw that has been dried in the sun and made into bricks.

ancient – very old.

engraving – a picture or design that has been cut into a surface.

thermal – using heat.

Online Resources

Booklinks
NONFICTION NETWORK
FREE! ONLINE NONFICTION RESOURCES

For more information on
deserts, please visit
abdobooklinks.com

Abdo Zoom
DATABASES
BEGINNING ONLINE RESEARCH

Learn even more with the
Abdo Zoom STEAM database.
Visit **abdozoom.com** today!

Index